About the Author

Samson Yung-Abu is a modern motivator, creator, mentor and tutor of people around the world. He is best known for his trademark motivational quotes distributed through social media platforms around the world. He is the author of *Student Exam Passport, Snacks for Thought, It Was a Time When* and *The Creative Talents Notebook*. He holds a master's degree in psychology from Nottingham Trent University and a bachelor of law and criminology degree also from Nottingham Trent University.

You

Samson Yung-Abu

You

Olympia Publishers
London

www.olympiapublishers.com
OLYMPIA PAPERBACK EDITION

A CIP catalogue record for this title is
available from the British Library.

ISBN: 978-1-80074-651-0

This is a work of fiction.
Names, characters, places and incidents originate from the writer's im-
agination. Any resemblance to actual persons, living or dead, is purely
coincidental.

First Published in 2022

Olympia Publishers
Tallis House
2 Tallis Street
London
EC4Y 0AB
Printed in Great Britain

Dedication

To every kind and loving soul on this planet. You know who
you are.

Acknowledgements

Thanks to everyone who has made this book possible.

There are no limits if your heart is in it.
Love is an adventure of hearts, and poetry is its atlas.

Love is all about making each encounter count, making each story into a wonderful history. Creating moments better than the previous, and sticking together no matter what the sky drags in; the good, the bad, the ugly, the better, the worse and everything in-between. Love is moving on from our history and forward into the future. Not with our past mistakes, but with the lessons derived from them.

For when we lose sight of the lessons in our love history, we lose sight of our true strength. We lose sight of prevention. We lose sight of advancement. We lose sight of positive conversion. We lose sight of self-acceptance and self-love. We lose sight of self-resolution. We lose sight of blessing. For history is the blueprint to victory. History is a sign of hope, of betterment, of how deserving you are to rise above your darkness into your own sunlight.

Acknowledgement

You is for you. From me to you. The story might be different than ours, but the scenery in it reminds me of you. Thank you for the good times, thank you for the bad times, thank you for the better times to come. Here you go, read *You*. My one and only you.

What Is Poetry?

In a few words, poetry is the atlas of all kinds of emotions.

Poetry is on a slow rise again in present years, and this should be of no wonder. We now live in a health-burdened society, where regardless of poverty or the prosperity of the city, millions of souls are constantly sad, helpless and depressed. Not just physical health but mental health. And as it turns out, people are feeling more negative because the positive of an advanced world has shaped our perspective in a poisonous way. It has made it so that we have to feel less when we have less than our neighbours, making us crave a life that demands us putting our mental health at risk to attain a life not compatible with ours. This is what makes poetry a suitable means of mental reset when life upsets us to a point where we feel lost.

Poetry engages with the empathetic side of humans. Despite it being an ancient mode of intimate interpretation, in recent years it has accelerated the pace at which young people can engage with themselves and with one another. Poetry is relevant because it dives beneath the skin and into the soul of anyone with a beating heart. Poetry is about making effective use of emotions. It gives intense emotion a sense of meaning. Why am I feeling this way? Big question. A burdened question, burning us out day in and day out, draining us of the ability to want to do things.

Poetry takes your question and turns it into an explanation. The truth of the matter is, most of us are silent about what we are going through mentally because we struggle with understanding our feelings. And in doing so, we struggle to express them. We fail to explain them in a way that we can confront them. We can't solve a problem we can't explain. Poetry provides a picture which serves the advantage of giving clarity to the writer or the reader, to the speaker or the listener.

This makes poetry magical. It helps us vocalise what we can't put into a day-to-day way of talking with others. It helps us navigate our negative feelings in a way that brings out light and positivity in others when they begin to read it. This is because people are reassured that they are not the only ones going through such gory thoughts and that we can reach a stage of glory no matter the gloomy clouds we encounter in life. We just have to rise to the test of confronting them instead of conforming to the silence it inspires in us.

What has poetry got to do with love?

Love is vulnerability and brevity all in one. And despite our vulnerable moments, poetry is valuable because poems, like polaroids, capture our emotions in their brevity and purest form.

As you will find out in this wonderful book, love helps us

enjoy the benefits of the beauty in each moment of life, despite the historical burden in our lives. As we might know, love is a rollercoaster of beginnings and ends—highs and lows of emotion. But the magic of love can't be fully expressed without poetry. The pinnacle of love can't be fully achieved without poetry. Love is an adventure of hearts, and poetry is its atlas.

Why is this book written in a story-like form?

It's pretty simple: apart from stories having the ability to entertain, they have the power of enlightening their reader. In short, a story is a wonderful way to teach wisdom. Stories are magical, and they can be used as a device to influentially distribute wisdom to their readers.

About This Book

This is a short verse, poetic novelette about elements that make a relationship work at its best, support a relationship through its worst and revive it to something much better. With great reluctancy, I left out some details such as names, ages, numbers, locations and cities. I wanted to give the story a sense of anonymity, so it could be about whoever you want it to be. Perhaps, it will make the book more personal and relatable to my readers.

Author's Note

Being romantic is not a weakness. It is what love demands. It is the vase of water in which the stem of love settles in and blooms through. Romanticism is the lifeline of lovers. Therefore, being romantic is the terms and conditions to keeping the love alive!

Dear You,

If you are already in love, this book is for you.

If you need to be loved, this book is for you.

If you are still in search of love, this book is for you.

This book is a must—give or take.

Yours truly.

P.S. There is a Joe Goldberg lesson in this book. Thank you, Caroline Kepnes, for inventing his character and chaos.

Love at First Stroll

You trip into me, and
you catch your breath as I
catch your body. The world
stops spinning like a wheel—
finally. My soul takes a rest
from the wheels of loneliness.
I smile, wholesome.

You look into my eyes,
your gaze steady—catchy.
I hold you firm, but my legs
feel rubbery, and earth
suddenly feels slippery.

I am unable to walk away.
You are unable to look away.
You separate your lips
to catch your breath again.
I am drawn in, captivated.

You close your eyes
as if enjoying a
peaceful melody.
I close mine as if
enjoying a wonderful long kiss.
Our souls go on a stroll.

Lucky Strike

"Hello there," I say to you,
my introduction of interest,
the first word in the chain
of event of lovers.

Your eyes unfold
on me like dawn,
as my hands are still
settled on you like dusk.

As if in sync, we unleash
our gazes without a flinch,
letting them attach themselves
to one another. In an instant, my
heart sheds away its sadness
as you glint like the first sunrise.
I glare through both windows,
unashamed, mesmerised.
Fixated.

You smile a trademark,
and in that millisecond, your smile
gives me a million reasons
to fall in love with you.

My heart immediately
spins like a roulette, and
the balls inside my
eye sockets settle on your smile.
Jackpot!

Your World

I look into your eyes,
and my feet float free
as your gaze takes
me past my deserted,
loveless shorelines,
away from the sand
and the seashells into
your ocean of spring
warmth. And I can feel
myself immerse into
everything you are made of
from head to toe.

I have never felt
space this free, calm
this simple, peace this
pretty, waves this high
and tides this wonderful
before this moment.

This is it, I think to myself!
You are it! My butterfly
reassures me with endless
flutters, as my soul sings
to the beat of my heart.

I am not sure about many
things, but I am certain
about a few things: love,
happiness, purity, endlessness,
eternity, the right one, you.

I look at you deeply:
your eyes, an ocean of calm;
your face, carved and crystal;
your body, breathtaking and beautiful.
Your demeanour, deep and daring;
your smile, exotic and explorative.

I dive with every being,
bone and blood that makes
me mortal.

My heart dips heavily,
my feet float freely,
my hands feel wet with treasure,
submerged, pulling me in,
waiting for you, I and us
to emerge into one, love.

I am deep, and I don't
want to ever float up to the
surface where my shoreline
is in sight again. I have found
a new peaceful place tucked
right at the centre of my
planet.

Please Be

You smile again, and
your lips unfold further,
holding me in
like an empty bowl
and filling me up with endless
desire my own world couldn't fulfil. Love.

I think to myself, *Are you taken?*
Please be single, I plead inwardly.
You take my gaze in, and
my question withholds.
You take your lips apart expertly
and reveal a single smile.
Right there, you confide,
letting me know your current
status. I can picture myself
filling that promising
vacant position.

I smile a relief as worry relieves
itself from my creased brows.
Right then, my soul stretches to life,
ready to mingle with yours.

"Thanks," you whisper

as you steady yourself.
My hands still fitted
around your shape.
Your eyes still fixed
flawlessly on mine.

You retreat a little and
smile shyly. "I am okay,"
you say to satisfy my worry.
I relax and smile at
the tone of your voice,
certain and soft against my
ear like an assuring yes,
like a whisper of endless
promise of eternity.

Green Beauty

I look at you, and I
see your face, more than
beautiful, more than flesh,
more than carved, more than
crystal. I crave.

Your face is a pristine
lawn, a garden of beautiful
features with many pretty
flowers.

Your green eyes, stretched
towards me like steady
branches with green fresh
leaves, and I can tell,
your beauty is parallel
to the garden of Eden.

Without the usual hesitation,
you lean in for a hand
shake, and I smell your
scent like a bouquet of roses.
You remind me of a path
never travelled, your scent
asking me if I fancy a journey.

My End Game

I have never seen the stars
and the moon this close,
this gorgeous, this glint.
You smiled a world, making
the universe so small,
its 7.7 billion people unsuitable
for this encounter but you.
With that smile, you make whole
my soul, building me Rome
all in one sight. My heart, a
place long misplaced now
in place. I can feel its beats
in sync with your every breath.

You remind me of tomorrow's
purpose, hope. I need a
strategy, an end game.
I need you. I want you to
be my every city, my every
mile, my Rome, my Paris,
mi *amore*. I want you beside
me, talking crazy stuff about
love, about life, about adventure,
trekking the miles, measuring
it by nothing but eternity, listening

to birds chirp like the latest
pop music.

I want to wake up each day
and walk endless miles—hand
in hand through your smiles—
and climb your mountains at
night and navigate through
your every fortress, getting
found in your breath, in your
lovely eyes. I want to swim
beneath the depth of your
ocean, getting lost like a tiny
coin where all things stay
forever. I want to ride the
wave and join with you wherever your tide rides.

Butterflies

Inside my palm, your
hands feel like well-fitted gloves, your
skin feels fabric-soft and
summer-warm.

You retreat your delicate
hands, but your handshake still lingers inside
my palm, flowing into my
pumping heart like blood
in a vein. It has found its
way into my soul, breaking
down my I-will-never-find-someone-to-love facade of
what feels like a decade of
caged insecurities.

I can feel you,
your soul on my skin,
the glow in your gaze as
it sinks gracefully into mine,
making my soul pounce to life.

Feeding the butterflies starved
and growling for decades,
an insane longing that has
been made to fade and wane

miles away, by many exes
like a flame blown away,
on a highway, far away.

You, My Purpose

I look at you, and I
realise my true purpose. You.
I want to put you in my
heart already like a vase
and water you with every
drop of love that flows
through my vein.

I want to keep you
alive for me: keep you
wanting, breathing,
root-wet, blooming.

You smile at my smile
as if it were a perfect
performance, and I
feel your approval at
my action as if it were an
audition.

I Got You

Your phone rings,
and we both gaze
at the screen.
Sorry, I am nosey, but
I love to be next to
you, in your space,
for as long as I am
allowed to surface.

Your hands shake.
On the screen, it shows 'Ex',
and you hover your delicate
finger between the pick up
button and the hang up button.

You look at me as if
unsure, waiting for a sign.
I've got it. I've got you.
I press the hang
up button for you, for us.
You smile, playfully, pleased.

Me. No Ex. No Next

There won't be any ex
or next, I think to myself as
I see all the uncertainty,
insecurities, pain, need—scars left by
your ex—in how long it
took you to stop and
speak to me, to choose
between picking and hanging up.

I look at your palm, and
all I can imagine is all
the wonderful lovers'
language we will speak
through that little device
called a phone: the endless
amount of phone calls,
voicemails, kissing emojis,
heart-shaped emojis and
naughty winking emojis. I grin.

A Drink

I introduce myself by my
name, and your name floats
out right after mine.
"Pretty name," I say.
"That makes the two of us," you say.

The first drop lands on
you, and we both look
at the threatening cloudy sky.
A bell chimes, and we both
look at a couple leaving
the bar across from the street,
hand in hand, pulling each
other towards a wonderful
affectionate afternoon.

We look at each other shyly,
as if to confirm what we
both want. A smile is
all it takes, and we know that
you and I need a strong
drink and warmth, and to
get to know one another.

Inside the rustic bar,

you slip into your chair
opposite me so nothing
else can distract our view.
I love your idea, I think
you are a romantic genius.

The music speaks to us about
treating love like a baby
in need of care and affection,
and we listen like new parents.
It is a country song, I can't
really tell whose voice it
is but the lyrics seem fit for
this encounter.

Mesmerising

"I love the smell of your
cologne," you say.
"I love your scent," I say.

You unzip your lips with
one swift motion, and a
laugh pours out. It is the
sound of one enjoying oneself.

"You are the most exquisite
feminine I have ever encountered,"
I say as I scoop your gaze in. Tasty.

You shoot me a soft look while
your fingers play with the metal
hoop dangling from your earhole.
"I know it sounds asinine, and
insane, but I mean it," I say.

Your gaze shines as your face blushes.
"I am swoon," you say; the
whites of your eyes glow
like fresh snow, as they hold my gaze
like buttons on a T-shirt.
"I am glutton
for you," I say, giving you my
cleanest smile.

Voice

There is something
more about this
moment with you
in it… it feels eccentric.

It isn't the metallic
sky outside, or the romantic
song, or the exotic western
accent you breathe
into fresh oxygen or the
way it sounds to my
British ears.

It is the soul-soothing,
released sounds
between those red parted lips.

I paint a picture of you in
my future, and it is like the
brightest sun I have ever
seen in my whole life.

For a minute or so, I wander off.
To somewhere weightless,
someplace where everything

floats in the air, and nothing
settles. Somewhere where
you can see the moon and
feel like you can touch it
with bare hands.
Somewhere sensational
and mesmerising.

At that moment, everything
floats clearly around me.
In that moment, I realise
that I don't just want to
give you the things you
deserve but also the
things no one else is good
enough to deserve from
me—but you.

You wave in front of me
with a delicate hand, pulling
me away from a different
planet back into reality.

You gaze at me, holding
my full attention, freezing
the moment. Your hazel eyes
spoilt with amusement.
"Good to have you back
from dreamland," you
murmur playfully.

"It was worth the dream,"
I say, confessing in one
single breath.
"It was about you."

You reward me with
a sweet smile, a blush
and a tug of a blonde strand
of hair behind your ear.

"In that case, you are
off the hook," you say
shyly, without switching
my gaze with anything else.

We both smile.

You have this unapologetic
femininity about you. Falling like
rain drops, making the
atmosphere green and alive.

Your voice feels full of the
expectation of a sold-out
festival. Full, eruptive,
energetic and vibrant.

Fascinating, how you make
the wings of my butterflies
dance with delight, at each tone
you string from your slender

throat. How each sound
you emit makes the pit of
my stomach flow with glow.

With each breath you take
between each syllable you
make, my soul flutters and
stretches straight to life like the
strong wings of a plane
balanced in the sky.

The Future

My eyes walk down your
body like an aisle, and I
drift with desire. The kind
of desire where a holy man
stands behind us at the altar,
with a cross. You are in
bright fabric, I am in
black attire, and we touch
a Bible while uttering words
that end with a 'YES, I DO'.

You bite a chunk off your
little cookie, and my inside
feels like campfire. Lit.
I bite my lips.

Your head turns to the right.
I trail your gaze quickly as you
look over at an elderly
couple camped around a
little table, laughing and
chatting, dissolved into
one frozen moment.
"Isn't it such a polaroid
moment?" I enquire, looking

into your wonderful eyes.

You flick a sweet tear
off your cheek and smile.
"Aren't they cute and wonderful?"
you say.

I glance over at their
table again, at the catalyst for
such a wonderful wet affection.
Two tall glasses of latte sit
half-drunk. A newspaper
folded on one side, the
elderly deeply engrossed
in each other's gaze, buried
under the spell of lovers'
wisdom and love.

I nod a yes and smile,
quicker than a camera click.

The elderly man's right
hand descends on her
face, lit under a hazy lantern,
and tugs a strand of grey-brunette hair behind her ear.
She smiles. She leans in briefly
to give him a kiss.
You look engrossed.

"This is what society
doesn't see," you say.

"Isn't this what love is really
supposed to look like:
magical within and from away?" I say.

"Look at them. Old and happy.
Wrinkled but still
mingling, in love," you say.

"I know we shouldn't
judge a book by its cover,
but even if this were just a
cover, it is a great age to
find it worth it," you say.
I smile.

The Power of Love

"The discrepancy of society, huh?" I say.
"Yep," you say.
"How sad that society believes
that love is inconsistent," I say.
"Love is not inconsistent,
it is just a pattern," I add.

You nod a yes.
"Even though I have been
hurt by many flames, I still
believed that there is a flame
for me out there," you say.

"You are right," I say.

"I have gone through hell too."
You take a deep breath.
"Unhealed heartbreaks,
but when life makes your heart
hell, you don't just crack, crash and
burn down, you come out
a survival, alive, smoking hot,
better, taller, stronger, sexier
and tastier," you say, your face
serious and relaxed at the same time.

"So, you do believe in love like I do?"
I ask.

You smile. "Yes, I do, just
as much as I believe in the
power of self-love," you say.

"To love yourself is the
foundation of a constant joy," I say.

Your eyes twinkle at those words,
as if I just read your thought. The
words 'foundation' and 'constant joy'
excite you. I can tell by the
sparks in your eyes as your breath
rises with excitement at
the mention of those words.

You take a deep breath, and I
am pulled in by your scent.
"Awareness of self-love is a
modern necessity," you say,
and I smile. You are so
authentic, so eccentric, you
have this magnetic pull.

"Do you believe that some
people are unlovable?" you ask.

"Nope," I answer. You smile.

"Me neither," you admit.

"I think there
is a you are mine and I am
yours for everyone. Love
is a curse from birth
but a good, powerful one," I add.

"What makes you think that?" you ask.

"Because everyone is born to
love and to be loved," I answer,
simply and sincerely.

"So, love is prewritten,
destined?" you ask.

"Yes, we need love to survive
alone or around others,
to cope with flaws, to accept us
for who we are and who we want
to be."

"So, in essence, love overrides
judgement, huh?" you say.

"Yes, because love overflows
with joy," I say.

I look into your gaze, once more,

and my future shines with bright
crayons. I want to paint a lovely
future with you from scratch.
I want to grow older with
you and grey with you and sit
in our nook with a book full of
memories about all the colourful
things we have done before the
colours depart from our body and hair.

What's Love in One Word?

"So how do you define
love in one word?" you ask.

"Hmm, in one word,
love is work," I say.

"Work?" you ask, your
brows crease a little
as you wait for an
expansion on the
word 'work'.

I open my mouth and
it pours out like this.
"Everyone is entitled to love
and to be loved. But just
because you deserve it
doesn't mean it is going
to be easy. And now, I
don't know if I am going
to ever get it all right,
but I know that
I have the right to do it.
To love someone right
because I know that we

all deserve to be loved right.
We just have to work to
get it and then work more
to keep it."

You smile. I release a
held breath.

"Okay, so what about you?
How do you define love?"
I ask eagerly.

You pour. "Love is a lot
of work, I guess same
as you but with an icing
on the cake; fun.
When you have work
and fun, it becomes like a
hobby, a burning passion,
a healthy obsession,"
you say with a smile.
"But let's both expand on
love, it's fun together. I
will go first," you add.

"Love is more than patient,"
you say. You wait for a
few seconds. "This is where
you say something too," you add.
"Oh, okay. I get it now," I say.
"Love is a commitment," I say.

"Love is more than pain," you say.
"Love is pleasure," I say.
"Love is more than discretion," you say.
"Love is a trophy," I say.
"Love is more than a burden," you say.
"Love is weightless," I say.
"Love is more than a taking," you say.
"Love is selflessly giving," I say.
"Love is more than preference," you say.
"Love is compromise," I say.
"Love is more than rare," you say.
"Love is right everywhere," I say.
"Perhaps love is here," I say.
You smile, an agreeable smile.

Your hand hugs your
mug of coffee, and you
pour spring water down
your throat. You blush.
I watch you as I chug
mine down. I blush,
ambushed by butterfly
feelings.

You look over again at the
elderly. I can see it in your
eyes. You love such encounters
because they count the
most, during a recount
of the day's event.

You are not the kind of
girl people meet on
Craigslist. You like natural,
phenomenal, like the
conjoined twins,
like eclipse,
like love.

I want to be old and
wrinkled and happy and
in love with you one day,
I think to myself.

I look into your eyes and
I see the end game, infinity.
I would do anything to win
you a world of your wishing.

If I could right now, I would
snap my fingers to bring
you into your own version
of what's in your view.

I just need to play the right
tune, then get the tone right,
then get us in stone so that
I can roll a bright stone onto
your finger.

The Big Question

It is almost nine, the day has declined,
the sunshine has resigned,
the skyline is now inline
with dinnertime, it is time
to cross the fine line,
I have to say it this time.

I think of a punchline,
huge as a headline.
To align what's divine
to what's destined to be
mine. You.

I take a sip of my wine
and let it wash my
heart to the surface.

"I want you to be my girlfriend,"
I say with a straight spine,
breaking the ice.

You give me a visual smile
claiming me from
all realms of heart-breaking.

My ice melts, and my distress
undresses itself, its veil
falling away like the walls
of Jericho and sweeps away
like a strong tsunami.

I watch your smile stretch
around your lips, and
my heart beats
for what feels like forever.

You lean in closer into my orbit,
and your breath escapes and
intertwine with mine.
Your beauty is so divine.
My soul feels refined.

Wishful Thinking

"I loved the elderly
couple we saw today
at the bar," you say.
"How they smiled,
laughed and eased
into the moment like
teenagers, oblivious
to age," you add.

"I think it is the right way
to be human, enjoying
every moment of maturity
right," I say.
"Yes," you answer.
"This is how life should
be, you know, like living
life on your own terms
while you are still alive,"
you add with a shy smile
and a steady gaze.

"One day, we will wake
up not old or stressed,
perhaps not even sick, but
hanging on to our last

breath. While death is out
of patience, waiting to claim
us, and us, wishing that we
had more time to get up,
to go for a stroll, visit a
friend, smile at a stranger,
save an animal on a highway,
hug a tree, love ourselves
better, eat a favourite meal,
wash it down with pleasant
drink. Feel the sand, the
ocean, the wave and the
wind one last time.

"Wishful thinking, I know,"
you say as you smile.

Goals have no restriction
on what they can be,"
I say. Your eyes sparkle
as I look at you. "I dig your
wisdom," I say. "It is sexy AF,"
I add. You blush. Right
then and there, I become
certain I want to live life
with love, with you in it.

More Than

You are one of those girls
who don't go looking.
You are a treasure. You
just let faith draw the
one to you.

I feel like a pirate, a
conqueror of
Great Sea. You are not
just a one-night stand
or a one-time hook-up.
You are a book I want
to keep on my nightstand
and read and cherish for
life. With every other girl,
I have always looked at
what I could get. And what
they could offer. With you,
I am looking at what I can
sacrifice. With you, I am
looking at what I can
become. A husband.
A great man, a great
human.

I chew my third slice of
pizza, wallow it and
swallow it. You are
a helluva girl.

"We now have a baby," you say,
tugging one of your shiny
blonde strands behind your ears.
I smile at the confusion on my face.
You notice. You smile.
"It is called love, silly," you say.

I smile. "I want to be
everything for you—a
man, a hero, a friend, a shoulder,
a partner-in-crime. I want
to be everything with you,
a trust-worthy
lover, an ally, a family,
a parent, everything," I say.

"But let's start with being
a good parent to love,
our first-born," you say cleverly.
"We are going to be
great parents," the words
dance out of my mouth
and over the music.
You nod your agreement.
"I am so excited," I say.
You sketch me a beautiful

smile and paint my sky
with many stars; colourful
and bright. I can picture
the future in many beautiful
frames, hanging on steady
walls held by steady straight
strong nails, bright like flames—
filled with you in it, and me in
it and us in it.

At night, we put on
a pop mood through the
Bluetooth speakers,
and let the lyrics take the lead.
You smile and I smile,
and we encourage our
legs to stand. Our hearts
now floating in love,
our feet feeling fly.

You, me, in this moment,
skin to skin, the little animals
in our stomach awake
like morning birds, leaving their nest,
feeling free, fluttering wild
into a sunny sky, our bones
bloated with excitement,
our tongues, holding hands,
our breaths freezing time in place,
our brains creating memory,
our gazes shut, dancing wild,

our body swaying like gentle wind,
our hearts beating like speakers,
our soul glowing like
ballroom disco lights.

Mirror Memory

Yesterday, we fought,
and today, we are sat opposite
each other, our love stretching
too thin, suddenly too strained
to spin our soul like it
usually does. Then music
changes, waking our soul.

Through the speakers,
Justin Timberlake takes
charge, as his lyrics
take me like a magic wand
down memory lane with mirrors,
like a mirror I overlooked
yesterday. Love is a memory
mirror, and I am made to remember
this once again. I look into it,
hoping to see my reflection,
still a better man, still a hero,
still a man deemed capable
of keeping a vow! But instead, I see
you in it, my other half, my
wholesome, and it dawns on
me that everything I want
to be for you, that everything I

wish to see me be through the
mirror is based on everything
I do to do better, to see you smile
whenever the mirror is held
up against my memory! Your gaze
shows me that the fight for us
is now, right here.

Even before I had you, officially,
I knew I didn't want to lose you.
At the first moment you tripped
into my catch, I knew I hit a
goldmine all to me.

And like a chest of treasure,
I know your worth, I know you
are the best worth my hands
ever held in itself.

I remember the jackpot
feeling I had held by your eyes,
unshaded to fade in front of your
pristine face from my existence
into your gaze, mesmerised by
your ocean, feeling space-free,
calm-simple, peace-pretty, wave-high and tide-wonderful.

I remember digging, until
you became mine. Until my
heart immediately spins like
a roulette, and the balls inside

my eye sockets settle on your
lips. I still remember till date.
I was just reckless with my
lucky strike for a moment.

Now glaring into the mirror of
memory, I don't want to lose you.
Not yesterday, not today, not tomorrow.
There is no place we can't go,
we couldn't go, but our separate
ways isn't one of them.

I leave my space and fill the
vacant spot next to you.
Don't sweep under the rug
what should be taken out
in a trash bag, I think to
myself. I must take my
ego out, and into the
trash bag, double twist
it into a tight knot then
take it outside where it belongs
because love demands
accountability and confession.
It expects a sincere admission
if we are to work. You look up at
me, your eyes the aftermath of
tears. "I am sorry for fighting
with you," I say.

I kiss your forehead and cute
nose, and your freckles shine
away yesterday's clouds.
My heart rushes with your sunshine.
I take a sigh of relief, I flourish.
A smile hangs on your face,
like tree branches, and I see
greens and red roses and blooms
and you, and my heart is a
wonderful world again.

Goldmine

"Hey, baby," you say, "is it
weird that every once in a blue
moon I look at you and the
saddened faces of our exes
come into view?" you ask,
followed by a smile. I laugh.

"It's okay, my yearn, my you.
I am a finder, and you are a
keeper. As humans, when
we win, we are bound to
review the memory of the
history that gifted us our
victory: us, our pasts, our pain,
our heartbreak, followed
by our gains.

"Our scars are cursed with
the memory of its history and
strength, its darkness and stars.
In victory, we are forever reminded
of pain and strength. Of grit and
grace. Of battles whittled down
by courage, overridden by faith
and love.

"You should know that no
matter our battles, no matter
the little that each defeat has left
us with, no matter the bruise, pain
and blame our knees have stood
on and held fast to like nailed
nails, in the name of defeat,

"we must live on and love on,
because even when we rise and
shine, even when we unfold
and fly, our uglies will continue
to remind us of the scars
that we must carry around
within us. But we are entitled to
fight forward, to love onward, to
rise and resume—even in our
consuming memory of battles,
even in our little, and continue
to capture our title, continue
to reign again like the kings and
queens we truly are, continue
to claim again what's right for
us even with bridged scars."

I hold onto you, you smile.
You are gold, and you
are mine, shovelled by
love into one role, into
one mould. Together, we

make the perfect team.
We are a goldmine. There
is nothing better than
making things happen
when everyone thought
one was done happening.

I improved, I learned to
appreciate what's priceless,
I learned to keep what's
precious, I learned to make
things happen. You are a
living, breathing proof of that.

Our endless love is our witness,
our wedding rings will soon
become a solid alibi," I say.
You look at me in your
finest smile, feminine and
infinite, twinkling bright like
a campfire, lighting my heart.
Undressing my lips into a
naked smile, illuminating
electricity into me. I ignite.
My butterfly glowing like fireflies.

Lovebirds

I have always been capable of love
but never loved. Until now, until you.
To be loved, my heart has hoped for.
To love, my heart has searched for.
And now under this bright moonlight,
as the loyal sky plays wind soft like Mozart,
I find myself at my happiest. I love how
the soothing wind rearranges our skin
with tiny goosebumps. I love these
mesmerizing moments with you.
I love as the space between us peels away,
as our skin touches smoothly against one
another, as our warm breath bonds.
I love it here as our eyes flicker like
bright stars, with the tip of our lips
inking love into our souls.
The narrative, titled lovebirds.
I love it right here. And right now,
as the elevator brings us to our summit,
and the moment submits us back to reality.
I wondered out loud, looking into your
diamond like eyes. "What might the moon
above us be saying to us from up there?"
"Look at these lovebirds, aren't they adorable, perhaps?
Offering one another what's dearest,
their soul," you replied, your lips full
like the full moon behind you.

Summer Dawn

One of the biggest tests in
life is living in it whilst alive.
You make me feel more than
an existence. With me in
your world, every dusk feels
mooned. With you in mine,
every day is sunset, blissed and
blessed. Together, I feel
more alive than the sky
on summer's dawn.

Quiet Dungeon

The sky is now open, but
dawn is still closed.
The spring robin
is yet to announce itself, and
the wind is faded, filled with nothing
more than a salient silence against
the closed curtains. But I am up
already, sinking as if standing in
quicksand; eyes rubbing, inked red,
gin breath, looking like a bin,
rocky and roughened. Heart
unstable, feet swaying,
mood a steep slope. The breeze
of depression blows sad dusts;
killjoy, strong, biting, cranky,
churning, breaking, pushing
me to the sharp edge.

I see the edge of surrender,
To open like a dark hole,
void of shallows, deep with
endless shadows, edging me
to follow, ready to swallow
me and all my swollen sorrows,
waiting to confine me into its

depth of total darkness.
I just need to quench the light
with a little more gin.
I just need to let go of both feet.
I just need to keep sipping my gin
till I slip over my stings, till I
ease into the fatal fall, where
a long-lasting sleep becomes
a grave of grace, peaceful.

My neck moves, as if cricked, as
the kitchen door opens, and your
shaved legs now covered in
yoga pants walk you in.
You wipe your face with the hem of
your sweatshirt, and I come into
your view under the light.
Suddenly, I feel like a piece of wood nailed into
another wood, firm, as my gin glass
hangs mid-air, an inch away from my lips.
You inch closer, your ponytail
hanging on your head like a halo,
its end swaying behind you,
your headset around your neck
whispering *Surrender* by Natalie
Taylor, one of your favourite
jogging music.

My heart jigs loud. *Oh, Lord!*
I take a jagged breath as I watch
your perfect eyebrows come

close to each other above
your gaze, filled with concerns.

I try hard to think of something,
but my drunk head pounds louder,
as if dunk in a truck racing through
deep potholes. "Hope
the jogging helped
with your writer's block?"
I ask in an attempt to divert,
to cover my dark mood with
a conversation rather than a white lie.
But, either way, I am doomed to fail.
I am transparent.

The vulnerability of my
masculinity is void of its
anonymity, and I know that
you didn't even have to mention it,
I can see it in your motion,
your sense of my museum of mess.

Last night, I was a happy chap
at the movies. We smiled and
chucked popcorn in our mouths
while we watched the latest
Fast and Furious. I almost
choked on a popcorn, it
was the funniest thing ever—
your words.
Today, that smile, that fun,

isn't on my face, so you know
that something doesn't look right.
You also know this because you can tell
a cloud from a sun or rainbows
from other grey areas in the sky
under our world, inside our
unwalled hearts. And right now,
my mood is like a lightless
glass wall, locked but see-through.

The tears flow, and I can't
deny it or blame it on an allergy.
I can't hide it because
the gin is in my hand, in my gaze,
on my smell, on my sloppy smile,
in my legs, in my heart.
I am drenched in dark mood!

Your eyes settle, fixed on my drink.
"What?" I say, my tone almost snappy.
I close my eyes for a second.
An attempt to trap in my sad tears.

I open my eyes, and my
shoulders slouch. "Sorry, babe,
I just needed a quick fix,"
I say in a regretful tone.

You sigh. "Drinking is not a
quick fix, it is not a remedy
to pain, it is a slow poison," you

snap back, your face serious.

You switch off your music,
the first sign that you are
about to take the reins,
that you are about to right
my ruins.

I look at you, and your
gaze lifts up towards
mine, strong like the wings
of kori bustard bird, and my
soul holds onto them, but the
wind is stronger for me even
though your love is firm to hold onto.

Your eyes descend back towards my gin.
You take the drink from my hands
and release it into the sink drain,
the ice cubes hitting the bottom
of the stainless sink, loud and recklessly.
"This will ruin you, us, love,
everything that makes us happy,"
you say, pointing at the sink,
then pointing at the bottle.

"This is what always happens
when I have these moods," I say.
"So, I just drink till whatever
Happens, happens," I add.

"Whatever happens!" you
exclaim, your tone angry, hurt.
"Listen to yourself for a
minute, babe! Whatever happens
happens is how we let things
happen that we could have
stopped from happening. You
have as much of a say in it, if you put
in more effort to control your
ship during any storm. Remember,
I am on your ship, and a
drink is how the sinking
starts. And if you sink, I
sink. I won't blink another
minute while I watch you sink,
not just because of
me, but because of us.
We still have much ahead
of us, all the many adventures
we have on our bucket list
to do. I am not giving up
on you, on us," you say.

A tear floats down my face as
I face the truth once again like
a clear sunny sky.

"I spent the first half of my
life believing that life is
what it is. That those born
into misfortune are doomed

to fail. That those born into
fortune, are automatically
born from birth
to bloom and flourish.
 But, being with
you, loving you, loving myself
changed everything."

You wipe your face.
"Now I understand that life is what
we make it to be. To fail or
to flourish is how well we
choose to love the little things
that we have now. How much
we care for them, how much
we nourish them to bloom full.
It is these little things that
decide our fate later on.
Not that," you point to the sink.
"Please don't let such little
misfortune ruin our little
fortunes," you say to me,
holding the half bottle of gin.

My mind goes blank as I
gaze at the rest of the bottle in your grip,
turned upside down, pouring out,
my liquid remedy making its way
down the same dark pipes.
You take a deep breath, you exhale.
"Are you going to be okay?" you ask.

"Nope," I say in blurred vocals.
"Aren't you going to work today?" you ask.
"I have no motivation today for
anything," I say. You come closer,
you hug me tight and, suddenly, my
weights are now almost light.
I feel released. I hug you back,
tight like a knot. I feel held.

"Babe, you can't
keep drinking your pain away,"
you say.
"But it drowns my pain,"
I say.

"Then they surface again,
stronger, meaner, pushier," you say.
You hold me. It feels as if
you can see my edge, edging
me to speed up. As if you
are a police car, pulling me
over on the highway.
I look away. I want to
speed to a quick escape. Death.

You turn my gaze to yours,
I look into them, and I see more
than tears. They are filled with
life designed for more
than one person. Slowly, I feel plugged-in.
I look into them, the safest

exit on the highway, and
I am unable to look away.

I know that all it takes
is a handful of this gin
which is in reality a
bunch of mixed chemicals,
and our chemistry ruins,
I think to myself. *That's*
how it normally ends. I know,
and I don't want that. The
thought of losing you is
worse than the thought of
losing myself. I want to
win so I don't lose you.
But how? I think it all to myself.

"Talk to me, damn it," you say,
breaking me from my thoughts,
both palms curved around both
sides of my cheekbone.

Ignoring the rising sun and
the stale air, and the chirping
of gracious birds piercing
through the curtains, I look
for a sunny smile on your
face, but I see sad tears glowing
under the sunlight. It hits me
in my guts. I am expecting
what I don't deserve right now.

"I know. I know drinking is
not the solution," I finally say,
my knuckles overstretched
over my skin. "It stings to be sad
and vulnerable at the same time.
But what hurts the most is
making someone who doesn't
deserve to be hurt by your hurt
get hurt by your reckless choices.
I hate this kind of moments,
the ruins of my infliction, of
my decisions. A self-inflicting
doom, destroying the day
of someone you love," I say out loud.

"Then stop the drinking,
please," you plead.

"But the pain. It's a lot of burden
to my heart. I just want to exit, it
is easier than to exist.
I want to avoid it all, the pain,
the past, the suffering, the
emotional pain from
depression," I say.

"Pain is not to be evaded,
it is to be evolved with,"
you say. "Don't let your past
enslave you, let it empower

you," you add.

"We as humans are often
blinded by our present frights, that
we fail to remember our past fights,
that we fail to see our present might,
that we fail to see our inner
light. But when we rise up to
the height of our might, we
are able to see the end of our
mountains in sight, then we
are able to surmount our fright,"
you say. "And the best part about
pain is that," you continue with
your most cheering voice, "its adversary is
an adventure when done by two.
For pain might be a curse,
but love is a blessing,
love is a cure.
I am in, are you?" you say, you ask.
I blink. I stay silent, shedding
renewed tears.

"Listen, babe, depression is
like an obscene graffiti
on a wall; even when you
paint over it, you still know
what's behind that paint," I say.
"I know that, I had it once
before, long time ago. But
here is a way out. You break

down the wall, you get help,
you rebuild a new one," you say.

"You had depression?" I ask,
shocked.
You shrug, a minor shrug. "Majority
of the world-wide population
did and do," you say. "I and
you, we are among the population,
we just have to figure out how
to live with it rather than without
it," you add.

You inhale, your
breath a spring robin chorus
to my ears, waking my slumbered,
reckless, narrow mind.
"I am here for you now, we
can figure things out together, without
the gin," you say, shaking the now-empty bottle.
"Let's try what we have. Us together," you say.
"Love, communication, even
therapy if we must," you add.
"But I don't have any motivation,"
I say. "I want to, really, for you,
for us," I add.

The pain surfaces again
like a growing grass, but
my hand is empty of my gin.
I look past one of our outdoor

picnic pictures, pinned to the fridge
without a bottle of gin in it.
I look at the cupboard where
another hidden stash hides for my
rough patch, but I hinder
myself from making
matters worse.

I weigh the pros and the cons,
and love wins in my heart. Gin lost.
Sorry, gin, you can go to hell all by
yourself.

I look into your eyes.
But with your tears visible,
I realise that winning requires
more than just weighing benefits,
more than the sink swallowing
by a quick remedy.

I kiss you, and you pull back,
your Mexican sunrise sky closed for magic.
You open your mouth, but nothing
comes out. Your chin rises again, and
your wet gaze meets mine.
Your face now an affection,
fighting with my infliction.
Your cheekbones open up again,
and this time, words pour out.
"I know deep down you really
want to feel good, but motivation

is an unstable friend in need,"
you say. "And right now, we need
to go on with what we have,
not what we don't have," you add.
You hold my hands
into yours softly. "How about
we try intention with dedication
rather than intention with
motivation?" you say.
I look at you, my sadness,
raining down, staining your
thumb wet.

"Please, babe, don't let the violence
of silence eat you alive.
You are not alone in life,
and at the very least, know
that you are available to be
there for you if you let yourself.
If you let me," you say. You look
at me and my wet shame
hides away from you. For once,
I wish this were Instagram,
where I could just filter my
shame into those million-likes smile.

"It is okay to fall on the journey
on the way home," you say. "And
when you do, you don't hate your
feet, you don't cut them off. You tie
your shoe lace, you get back up,

you dust your being, you wipe your
knees. You keep on going despite
the bruises, despite the pain,
despite your pieces, you
plough on, till you can find
peace to heal, till you get
home," you add.

I take a deep, jagged breath,
like a prey on the run, injured
and scared as my emotions
roar like many mighty
predators for what feels like
the umpteenth time. A smile
fights on my suppressed, closed
lips. That usual weightless,
feather-like, flattering smile,
now heavy, deflated, flat, fatal on my
face, even when forced.

Even fake knows when it
cannot mimic what's absent—
happiness. *I have indeed reached
my limit of joy,* I think to myself
once more.

You pull my chin up to your
gaze. "We are made in the image
of the one who did all things good,
who made all things bad
greater, who conquered death and

rose high. We are already
strengthened, we are already
made winners, even before the
war within us was made.
If we keep worrying about the
past or other people's negative
judgement on us, we will always
say no to our own joy even if it is
right in our hands, even if it is
right at the centre of our hearts,
and in our sight," you say, blinking tears,
and placing a palm gently
on my chest.

"Look, I love you, okay?" you say.
"More than leaving you would
ever make me feel," you add.
This hits me hard! I nod, and my heart
trumpets in triumph. "For a long
time, I have been misunderstood and
taken for a fool. But with you, with love,
I don't feel like a tool any more. I feel great!
My smile celebrates
victory over my sadness, as all my
numbness is replaced by your
stress-less ease.

I look at you again, my
drop-dead gorgeous, and the
walls in my eyes fall and
crumble beneath me. Your

eyes rise up like a tall mansion, and your
sight inhabits me, and my
heart takes flight into the light.
Once again, my dark emotions in their
relentless attempts echo
like giant feet, trying to overtake
the miles of my smile, but you
silence them with a lightning-speed white shine.

It is true, love is light,
love is might, love is the
very height of all sight.
Even in my vulnerability,
you see vitality; even in
my stupidity, you see sensitivity;
even in my negativity, you see positivity;
even in my insanity, you see serenity;
even in my naivety, you see brevity.

Now away from the edges
of persuasion and self-prosecution,
I can see the passion to live on,
I can feel inside my heart,
beating boom. The room feels lit,
and my dark mood wades
without any hesitant haste.
My joyful smile looms.
And now, my heart, previously
a jungle of dark thoughts, is
now peaceful like a
quiet dungeon.

Love Taught

You've strengthened
my soul. You've made
me realise that love is
the strongest foundation
of affection and passion.

Loving you taught me
not to lose my head
even when I've lost my
footing at the steps of life.
Not to lose my heart in
the heat of the storms,
even when I've lost my
gentle emotions momentarily.

Diamond Time

Today, your essence
signifies my presence
as my soul feels soaked
like in a hot summer sun
as your kiss tans my lips.

I hold you into my palm
like beach sand: soft,
soothing, free. You smile,
and my soul pulls to the
depth of your ocean, your
soul. I glint anew like a freshly
cut diamond.

It is true, with time you
can turn a dime into a
diamond and pain into
profit. My loss left me in
a dime but the pain
prepped me for this
diamond moment: you.
You are my diamond time.

You. The Joe Goldberg's way.

"I am having a freaking
bad week," I say, my
breath heavy, my
shoulder a mountain,
my soul a dehydrated soil.

I put my sketchbook
down, and immediately
you close your *You Love
Me* copy, and put your
characters to bed. *Sorry,
Joe; sorry, Caroline Kepnes,
it's my turn to be loved.
We all want attention
like Goldberg does,
we all need love like
you've given his character.*
I think to myself. You pull
me into you and assume
the role of a shoulder to cry on.

You drip me with smiles
and pull me in. My soul
absorbs.

I fold onto your chest,
your softness
and fragrance a
consoling cradle.

You kiss my nose, then

you look at me, your
pretty freckles summoned
by the nightstand lamp.

"Listen, baby," you say,
your voice lullabied, a
soft wind. "A bad day is
like a puddle held in a
pothole, and a pothole
is only a tiny fragment
of the tarmac," you say,
your voice breezing into
my soul, dusting away
my sadness.

"And what happens when
you step into the puddle
in your best new pair?"
you ask, but not expecting
me to answer. I close my eyes,
I don't just want to hear your
words, I want to feel your voice.

"You don't stay in the pothole
forever, you catch your breath
and stop scratching recklessly
at your heart. You don't chuck
your shinys away either.
You step out of the puddle,
perhaps with a few nasty
words out of haste and

hanger, it's called being
human with a passion
for a perfect sunny day."

You tuck a strand of hair
behind your ear, I can sense
it with folded eyes.
"It's okay that you couldn't wow
the audience today. You
don't have to stay caged in
the puddle, or tattoo a badge
of shame on your face,
or waste another
age in rage, or read the same
sad page every other day. You
get grateful for the opportunity
to see the day, then you get off the
stage, you clean up the mess,
you dry your emotions, you fix
yourself up anew, you continue
to where you were meant
to be going. You come back
twice shy, wiser, better, braver.
A wower! That's how moving on works.
That's how you move on
with the rest of your
journey. With happiness,
with love for the adventure
and the destination."

You hold up the

You Love Me you
were reading earlier on,
the third sequel of Mr Joe's
tragic encounter with love.

It is hard to tell if Joe is
more the toxic one or
the romantic one, perhaps
both, but he sure makes tragic
look eccentrically easy
to pull off and get
away with it every time.
I am glad that we have
our own love story right here,
right now. I am glad I have
you.

You are more reliable
than all of Joe Goldberg's you's,
I think to myself in relief.

You shake the hardback
like a tambourine. "Moving
on makes all the difference, baby.
Like Joe Goldberg did after Guinevere
Beck, with Benji, Peach, Amy,
Delilah, Forty. After his
shitty potholes with trust,
with love, with happiness—
Joe kept on going. Joe is
like a mouse on a wheel,

active, motivated, crazily
hopeful."

I nod my approval.

"Everything about Joe Goldberg
can be broken down to two
things, hope and a longing
for permanent love," you say,
unfolding two fingers.

"And what did he do right?"
you ask before answering.
"He hoped for a better day
ahead, a fresh start.
He moved on. And okay,
sometimes he tried
to achieve the right things
with the wrong means,
but hey, hell yes, he did do!
And he strived. He thrived."
You look into my eyes, and the glow is brighter than the
nightstand lamp.

I open my eyes, I smile.
You look at me. "Okay,
I know Joe is kinda
toxic and borderline lunatic
when it comes to love, it's
his obsession with passion.
His deeds were more out of

a craving for positivity than
out of pessimism and his
gesture is somewhat exotic,
his sense of hope to better
is heavily heroic when it
comes to fixing love
and cleaning a mess on the
spot after he hits a pothole
filled with puddles of perfect ruins.

"You get what I mean?"
you enquire in one breath.

I nod a yes.

I close my eyes, not sure
of what to say, but one thing
I am certain of is that you
have a unique way of making
anything make sense to my soul.
You shed light on any shade.
You've made magic out
of Joe's tragedy. Like you've
made a better man out of me.
And now you've shined
my cloudy soul with your
soothing voice. I smile
for the first time tonight.
Way to go, buddy Joe,
I root from within my soil,
my soul.

I unveil my eyes, and yours
fall flawlessly into mine
like petals, and I bloom with
life anew like fresh roses.
I listen to your heartbeat,
and I feel held and released
at the same time. Contained
and set free. This is how you
make me feel—held, released,
contained and set free.
Loved and in love, cared and cured.

My heart unfolds further
as you kiss my lips. It is
funny how filled with
happiness and weightless
I feel. How unburdened. Your
wise words have washed
away my burden. These are
among the perks of being
loved by you. Of you learning
something positive from
Joe Goldberg's mens rea.

Valentine: Simple Things

It is valentine's night,
the breeze weighs light,
the moon is a kite. Hearts
are lit bright, hands are
held tight, as couples'
souls walk under the
lovely twilight.

I look up at the sky, and
I smile bright. The sunrise
has settled, and the sunset
is long gone, but the butterflies
within my soul are still a dawn,
full to the brim; my heart is
still buzzing, full with love,
still drawn in passion, still
drinking your love like a potion.

"Are we there yet?" you ask.
"Is it a restaurant? It is, isn't it?
I can hear clattering, and
I can smell something
delicious," you say, your
voice filled with delight.

"Yes, it is a restaurant,"
I say reassuring your
impatience. "But at a place
you've never been before,"
I add.

We enter, and I guide you
through the skylight
towards the booked table.

I untie your blindfold as
soon as I guide you into
your seat.

You open your eyes,
and your gaze measures
with pleasure. The
moment becomes a
treasure as your red
lips separate into a wow.
You twinkle for what
feels like a lifetime.

"I am glad I wore my
best black dress and
my favourite heels," you say.
Your smile as bright as
your shiny earrings.

"Why did you think I put
on my best tuxedo and

cologne?" I say, smiling.

"This is big!" you exclaim,
your gloved hand sliding
through the air in a wave,
your eyes taking it all in
like a camera. I smile.

"You are big a deal to
me, and I just want to
enjoy the simple things
with you," I say as we
both drench into the
display of our romantic
night.
The candlelight
sways as the music
moves like the wind
around the dinner table.

After a few bites, your
gaze falls onto mine,
warm and soothing.
I drink it all in. My
butterflies enjoying the
divine taste.

"This is super delicious,"
you say.
"The best in town," I say.
The music starts playing, and you

hum with delight. Your
head dances slowly to
the music as I sing
along *Simple*
things by Miguel to
you.

You smile your best
smile, and it hits my
latest heartbeat.
The magic of that
smile, pouring out so
simply, making my
heart make a big deal
out of it. It is magic how
a little gesture that
many might take for
granted can kite the
soul anew. I hold onto your
gaze like strings, floating
high with delight.

This is the effect you have,
this is the effect love
has. Love makes little
things matter in quality.

Team Love

Today, we have quarrelled,
and our souls have gone grey,
quiet. There are no limits if
your heart is in it? Right! That's
what I thought, but right
now, I feel like I am at my
limit with everything with you.

But even in our silence,
our hearts are shouting
from the side-lines,
yelling at us to get back to
treating each other as the
lovers we are.

You gaze at me with a smile,
your gentle smile, an accolade
which I currently don't
deserve. It rinses away the
barricade that I have built
around my heart. I realise
how flimsy my wall is,
how stupid I am to waste
all that energy on building
a wall in-between, whereas

I could have spent that same
energy and built a bridge to
get back to your side, and
love you like I should have.

Now that my walls have
fallen, I see the silence in
your eyes stretching into
mine, making my heart
beat like thunder during
a storm. Pulling me away
from the losing team, a
place I have chosen
in my haste of rage, a place
where I don't belong.

Now I see you, as love
yells at me to get it together.
I remember one thing:
Love is a coach, and you
and I, we, are on the same
team on the field, even
when our mood fails, even
when our souls fail to
match a sunny day, even
in my wreckage and your
rage and your cage and
my chaos, in our life, we
must find the courage and
strength to surpass our
stress, to rise, to regroup

to rebuild no matter
whose vantage point seems
right. It is what you once
told me. I took note, I
learned from all my previous
wreckage. We are a team
on the same side. I smile.

I will own up to my loss.
I am sorry. It is true, when
love is involved, there are
no limits if your heart is in
it to come on top as a winning
team.

Wife-Time

Nine months later,
we are still aligned.
Time after time,
you've proven to be mine.
This is a wonderful sign.

Despite our many faults,
love makes us flawless,
lighting us like zillion
stars no matter the darkness.

Isn't love the fairest?
Isn't love more than a tale?
Isn't love the fiercest of
all things mighty and mean?
Love the king of all hearts.
Love is the conqueror of
all hate.
Love does not let the happy
endings of fairy tales take
away the essence of the happy
endurance of love. Love is more
than long-lasting,
love is everlasting.
You are my love,

my forever,
I think to myself.

I recite the last few
months in my mind,
the memory rising and
shining like morning sun. I
realise that our relationship
is a test of many tears,
but through the
teary sky of tests, we've
done more than survive,
we've thrived as one.

On my toughest days, you've
shielded me. Your vulnerable
days have strengthened me as
I fought by you. Side by side.
Smile by smile. Hands intertwined,
heartbeats combined.

I am your knight and you are
my armour, we are impenetrable
against all teary battles because
love is a powerful weapon.
This is what calls for tonight.

Tonight is a fine night,
with dinner and wine.
I resigned from my seat so
I can be closely aligned

with you where you sit.

I lift you up and spin
you around. You twist
around until you settle
in front of my gaze. Now,
we are face to face, our hearts
in one steady race.

I lean in. Your lips intertwine
with mine, hot like
a smoking pipe, tasty
like French wine, divine.
"I want to make you my
wife," I say.
"We need an arrangement
before such engagement,"
you say playfully, your
smile pretty big.

Then you sign high.
You resign an inch,
"Are you serious?" you ask.
I nod like a devoted dog.
You smile, and it fills the
room with hype and vibe.
I feel alive.

Knowing You

You look fabulous
in your pyjama pants
and your Sunday bed
hair as you watch
me carve us breakfast. Sexy.

You saunter towards
me and plant a kiss
on my lips. "You
drank coffee without
me?" you ask playfully,
a smile shining in-between
your teeth.

"You wore me out last night,"
I say, then I follow
it with a wink.
"In that case, get more coffee,
because today, you are
all mine," you say.
I made you tea and a fried
egg in a sandwich.

You murmur in pleasure
as you chew every last bite.

"You know the way
to my heart," you say.

"I would be worried
if by now I didn't
know," I say back.
You wink this time.
And I think of how
lucky I am to have you.

Love's a Teacher

Over the months, you've
become the greatest test, and
I see my colours flying
each time you smile
bright. A plus. Love teaches
us a lot; about faith, hope, pain,
wisdom. With you, I finally
have faith in my feet.
I finally have hope in
my heart. I finally have
purpose in my veins.
I finally have wisdom
walking at your height,
head high, feet tight, light
bright, hearts gaining might,
watching love in full sight.

A Blessing

All my mistakes have
prepared me for this
perfection, this sight,
this moment with you
in it. You've made me
a home, framed in love.

Throughout the years, I
kept running into the next
girl, leaving my ex, making
further exes, but the effect
kept leaving me exhausted.

But you, you are
something different,
angelic, a blessing.
You evolve me
You excite me.
You respect me.
You exalt me.
You keep me pure
like an altar. I will
worship you forever.

Despite my cracks,

you loved the wreckage
racked up in me before
we hooked up like
they were yours.

You dealt with them
like they were your
baggage, your own
skin and scars, your own
thorns and storms, your
own bone and body.

You've made me see
past the victim to
the villain I can
become against
my sadness.

You cheered me when
I felt chained to my
doubt, stood by me
when I felt crushed,
pulled me up when
I wouldn't pull myself up.

I was having cold
feet until you came
that first day.

Now, I am certain
it was meant to be you,

my warm socks.

You, blessed with
the scent of saint paint,
you have washed over
my slate, cleaned my heart
out of any hint of my
exes' stains. You've filled every
dent back with your
decent demeanour.

You, the blueprint of
love, I have been inside
your heart now for what
feels like a decade. And
nothing seems to fade.
We are like new, even
after months of use.

You've taken me
to all the places I
never knew was
for love, showing me all
the things no one
ever thought I deserved.

You became my
parachute when I
fell from my crashing
plane into your sky.

You made me feel
the wind, the sun,
the spins, the thrill,
the bliss of gravity
without any repercussions
that your love couldn't fix.

You, an ocean with
joy, even when I
cried a thousand times,
you washed them away
with your ocean-like gaze
like they were all one
single rain drop.

In your presence, I
feel okay letting my
emotions float to my
surface, for you give
me joy in return, not judgment.

You took me out of
my hell and into your
heaven, your heart,
a place where hope
now holds many more
great feats. A place I
am finally able
to find my own fate.

Your heart has taught

me so much. I have learnt
to let go of my rage and
hate caused by the
ones who left me in
hell with scars too
burnt to heal.

Your love is a cure, it has
carved out the scars
like a wind clearing
out the smoke and burns
of a little flame.

"You are one wonderful,
strong wind. The strength
of a tornado is pale
besides your presence," I say.

You smile and hug me
like a lifeline, and my vein
works overtime as my heart
beats alive. I smile.

"What?" you say playfully.

"Your hug envelopes me
like a warm ocean," I say.

"Your kiss recycles my
heartbeat," you say.

*This is precisely why I love
you,* I think to myself. *The
purity in your love for
me. The effect it has on
mine.*

My love for you renews
each day like a clean slate
waiting to be painted with
more of your love. With
each touch of you against
my fingertips, my heart is
swept clean like a fresh slate,
and I long for it to
beat forever for you.

Insecurities

My insecurities are minimal.
When you touch me,
I relax inside my own skin,
knowing that your
skilful hands aren't
burdened with the
weight of the like
button on your phone.

Coffee

"Morning, handsome" you say,
delightfully bringing me away
from my train of thought, *you*.
The sound of your voice hums
wholesome through the windows
of my heart like the songs of
a beautiful morning bird.

"Hey, you! Morning! Slept well?"
I ask.
"Better than ever," you say.
"Breakfast will be ready soon," I say.
I push a mug of coffee towards
you, watching its rising smoke
flicker against your pretty freckled
face. You tip-toe and your lips part,
taking my tongue in. I drink your
tongue, and it tastes better than the
best morning coffee I ever had.

Love tastes different when
you've had a shitty taste of lust
all your life.

What's Love Without

We have faced too
much, gone through
different phases,
but love never left our
faces.

Despite the tears, we
are not ashamed to smile.
Despite the fights, we are
never ashamed to admit
fault. Love brings a different
kind of fear that is healthy
for a relationship.

We value each other, so
we don't want to lose one
another to someone less
better. You loved me enough
to walk barefooted when I was
shattered into tiny pieces.

I never walk out the door when
you have those explosive
mood swings. That's what
love does; it keeps us wise,

it keeps us apprehensive,
sensitive and appreciative.
It holds our true values, it tells
us that we deserve to stay
together even if we
choose to show crazy
more than a few times.

Love keeps us fearless to
dance in the rain in daylight,
despite the market crowd,
despite echoing chatters.
What's love without a pinch
of sanity, a hint of insanity, a
flinty spool of salt every now
and then? Love is sweet, love
is bitter, love is always in flavour
in our favour, bitter or sweet.

Trust

I will never forget when
you gave me my best
piece of advice with
those soft lips. "Remember
when you said that you
don't care about my exes,
that they can all go to hell
and rot there because
you trust me?" I ask.

You shimmer, nod, then
you smile.

Your words still resonate
in my mind. "Do you
remember the one I mean?"
I ask.
"In life, people are always
going to attack you no
matter what you do,
but they are inferiors, and
wise kings and queens don't
waste warriors on inferiors,"
you say.

"My God, you are such a
goddess. You are my queen.
Your brain is beautiful," I say.

"I know, babe," you say.
"Why do you think I read
all these books?" you say,
pointing at our long wall
shelves of books.

"Your intelligence turns
me on," I say. You twinkle.
I sparkle. I am on. Our clothes
dim. Damn, love is 360 degrees hot!

Spontaneous Mood

It is eight a.m. in the morning
and the sky is wet with
rain beating against the
roof top, stopping us from
going out.

We ordered McDonald's,
ate it for breakfast,
kept our phones off,
and watched *Breaking Bad*.

Later on, with egg
on the kitchen floor,
sugar on our faces,
butter on our hands,
flour on our asses,
we've made a
right mess. We watch
the smears with
smiles loaded on our
lips.

"What a mess," I say.
"But who cares," you say.
"We've baked and

made the best cake,"
we say in unison, licking
each other's lips like fingertips.
You look at me, and
your eyes are on fire,
setting mine like a forest ablaze.
We've had a blast!

I lick my lips and,
you bite your lips.
Pleasure triggers.

You arrange your hair into
a bunch after brunch,
and I smile.
You release your
ponytail after that,
and I smile.
I hold your legs apart,
and you smile.
You lie and your back
arches, and I smile.

You stretch your
neck all the way
back, and I smile.
We get to the main
course, and we smile.
You always have room
for more in the room,
I always have more to

give you in the room.

You untie your modest restraint
and I unleash mine,
and we forget about
our shame. Our tongues
twisted in one, and we
fumble and tumble in delight.

With each hand on skin,
our souls climb to
the surface of our throat.

You moan and
I groan, and our souls
tie themselves into one
hot knot.

Together, our bodies
reach their fate,
we come undone.

Sex

My mind travels back
to last night, a place
where our body
dominated the moment,
but our heart came out
a real champion,
a place where our need
morphed into one
and we intertwined after
the last drop of wine.

"Was it divine?"
I ask you with my eyes.

"You struck all my cords last
night," you say.

You push my chest
playfully.

"You were such a
naughty beast last night,"
you add, completing
the tide, answering
my unsaid question.

I wink, and you smile.

"Did I forget to mention
that I am a tigger?" I ask.

"Nope," you say. "You were
too busy telling me what a
tight goddess I am," you add.

The details are truly
in the desire.
You always have a way
of making me think of
nothing else but you.
You never fail to give me the facts.
You are so immodest
with your satisfaction.

Climax

The moon is full, and
your mood is bright.
I sit straight as you sit still
on me without your tights.

I stroke a finger on your
tight skin, and you make a
sound like a guitar string,
waiting for more to complete
the melody.

My god, that smile
is my climax. Before the
curtains come closed,
before the stockings
come off, before the silk
panties come off,
before all my clothes drop
dead.

That smile is my climax,
after you summit,
after the thrashing, the moaning,
the juddering, the feeling
of frenzy when we arrive

together, that smile when
you let your soul swim in
a pool of pleasure is so
exquisite and exhilarating
to experience. You are my
climax.

Made Space

I have swept all my exes off my
heart with a love broom
to make a lovely room for you.

The walls smell like you,
fresh paint.
No thoughts of exes,
no taints of mess,
but clean fresh scent, you.

Every day, I think about it
all, and each day the full
view of my thought is a
sunrise. You are my new
beginning, my clean slate.

I think about your framed
smiles and hang them
nicely on my present memory.
My cracked walls are now covered
with your pictures,
your smiles. You.
You are such a healer,
a fixer. A surfeit gallery
of seduction. A capturer of heart.

You Are My Best Vacation

Sex is one thing, but a
soulful time with you
in bed without souls
lying naked through our
raw intimate conversations,
undresses our emotions
to their skeletons is a
different level of climax.
It is like an adventure in a sea
in the world's best vacation spot.

Truth be told, we have
been to so many vacations
together, but the best is a quiet
time in bed with you,
wedged between whispery
love songs and music.
Limbs knotted after a nice
takeaway meal delivered
by us from our own kitchen.

My love drools at the
waterfall way your voice
pours into my heart through
your throat when you speak.

When you spread your lips
apart and talk about everything
you care about while I dive
in and listen to you, your
every sound; your laugh,
your tone, your breath,
your hum.

Love Wins Against Pain

"Are you all right, babe?"
you ask, your voice filled
with concerns.
"No," I reply, my voice burdened
with the tone of frightened storms.
"It's the past again," I add.
"You know, sometimes the
past hunts me with sharp
spears, pointed at the centre
of my peace, arrowing into
me, sparing nothing of pleasure.

"It hits so fast, unannounced,
it is a painful process, a
fortress of stress. I am cracking
under its pressure, bleeding away
my comfort, unable to shed away
sadness," I say. "But you've seen
me like this once before, you
know what happened. It will
go away with time," I add, in an
attempt to put you at ease.

You take the glint sharp off my palm
and replace them with your

own palms. My palms suddenly feel
less endangered, less burdened,
less broken, less wingless.

You lean in. "Listen," you say,
your voice soft but serious,
"one of the things that makes
us human is suffering. One
of the things that makes us
human is survival. But for
everything that makes us humans,
we need to continue to have the
love to live, to hope in better,
to do our best until we see a sky
much better, a sun much
greener, a cloud less grey.
Survival is all about resilience,
about resurrecting again the
strength to survive, re-emerging
darkness like we once did before.
That's what makes us the
ideal candidate to be worthy
of happiness: the fret we've
tasted, the battles we've seen,
the pain we've felt."

"No matter how much I try to
shake it off, my soul slumbers
in my storm, failing to fight
my demons," I say, looking toward
the home of defeat. The floor.

I failed, I think to
myself, but your eyes hold
onto mine. I can see your
soul armoured. The fighter
in your soul is awake,
ready to work, to revoke
my past back to its long-gone era.

"We are two hearts dripping into
one cup, making it overflow
in one flow. And when you
have less to add into the cup,
I want to be the one to make up
for it till our cup can overflow
again with two. So, I won't wait
till the past takes a toll on you like
before." You take a deep breath.

"We've been down that
dark tunnel before. It is
smeared with sadness, smells of
nothing good and holds nothing
useful but painful razor sharp
objects," you say.

We both look at the scars and
the sharp razor, and the shame
overflows through both skies.
But they never make it past
my chin, your thumb catches

the wetness, then your palm
wipes the rest away from my face.
"I won't spend another heartbeat
affording the past more time to
claim you in pain, to gain
from our time, to drain you
of life. It won't win this time.

"What can I do to help?" you ask,
your voice ever so smooth, your
presence ever so necessary.

"You being here reminds me
that the present is a wonderful
remedy against the past,
it is what matters the most," I say.
My heart smiles a banana shape.

"You know, we all have a painful
past, and the past is a powerful thing,
it gives us pain, but in so doing,
it gifts us with the power to endure
it, until we can survive it."

You hold up your phone and
press play, the Bluetooth
speakers come to life with *Survivor*
by Destiny's Child. A smile
clings unto my face for
a brief second. You have a
way of setting the

mood with the right music.
Music is the genie
of moods, I remember
you saying before.

You lift my chin onto your
delicate palm and claim my
gaze from the floor into yours.
"I mean, after all we've been
through, look at you and me,
alive, hearts beating, in love.
It shows me that we do have
the power to let go of the past
for it has given us the strength
to knot onto the present, to pull
into the future like one would while
climbing out of a hole, pulled
up by a thick rope."

You gaze at me, again, this time
with a calm depth, and seal my
cracks with a crescent moon smile.
I drift into your ocean, floating
away from my anchored past.
Like last time, you ship me
away from my shaped past
of sadness into your shielded
present with a single sharp smile.
I feel shamelessly happy.
I uncage my lips and
free all my teeth. You've

freed me. I look back into your
gaze, now unfazed about my past.
"I feel proud to be loved by you.
Your love has won against my
past, my pain," I say, smiling
for miles at last.

Serious

I have been around so
many sunshines over time,
hoping they will stay,
hoping they will support me
like I have stood by them
during their storms, but
instead, they fake smiles,
slam the door when
I make them better. Leave
me under a metallic sky
filled with endless clouds,
cold rain, scar thunders.
Leave me cracked like the
aftermath of an earthquake.
They shame my love, and
leave my heart in cracks
and scars.

"Though rumours have it,
they never got anyone
else better," you say to me.
"I checked after our first
encounter," you add.
I give you the did-you-know look.

"Don't give me that look,"
you say. "I was only curious,
so I checked." Your eyes glitter.

I smile. "I did the same
after our first encounter too."

You smile. You knew
I would.

I look guilty. I know.

"You did what I would,
and I did what you would," you say.
"Is there anything we wouldn't
do for each other, to stay
together?" I ask.
We smile, confirmed.

"But this is why you are
something else. You do
your research, like I did.
You take me serious.
Like I do," I say.

Different Shine

You shine different.
You burn bright and melt my
cracks like rubber and seal
my heart with your endless, pure love.
Even during my lows, you
glow up into a full moon.
Around you, I feel like I am
in the brightest room in the
hottest summer without a roof.

Having a Goliath Day

Today, you feel sad, and
I feel saddened watching
your vacant smile. Your
lips shut, unlike the sky
opened with rain. Your sky
is cloudy, and your tears drop
like raindrops. A box of half
Kleenex sits next to another
empty; one of the Kleenex is
wet, squeezed into a ball in
your delicate palm.

"Sorry for my state," you say.
"I am having a Goliath day,"
you add, with a forced smile.
You sniff, catching another wet
prisoner from your right eye.
My heart drips into my vein,
and I wonder if it is still blood
or tears oozing from each beat.

You sniff again, your eyes
flutter wet, red. The red patch
around both skies, gaining more
colour. I think about what to

say, but I don't know much
about positive talks like you
do. You are the guru, I am
just your gentleman, your
shoulder, your partner in fight.

But I do know that love
brings out the fighter,
the David, in us all.
I start the only way I can
think of. "You vs your problems,
who would you bet to win the
fight if it was on Bet365?" I ask.
"You know, this betting sport app,"
I add.
"Yes, I do know it." You take a
deep breath, I watch.
"And I would bet on my
problems, of course," you
say, your voice clayed with defeat
already. I switch it up a bit.
"Okay, David vs Goliath?" I ask.
You don't answer.
"Imagine if Bet365 was around
during that time, and you had
the chance to bet big money
on one of them, who would
you have gone for?" I ask.
Again, you sniff, you stay silent.
I continue, as you watch me.
Thank you, Father Bell, your

sermons when I went to Sunday
school in my childhood are coming
in handy now, I think to myself.
I snap out of the past,
back into your sight.
You look at me expectantly.

You measure my gaze, and
I hold your hands into mine,
reassuringly.
"Realistically," I start,
"the average person
would bet on the big, strong
and dangerous-looking one.
Given his history of violence
and status, Goliath was all of
that, plus an enemy," I add.
"We would always
bet on the problem because
it is bigger than us. But David,
he had the tools, he just needed
to step up and face the giant in front
of him. Nothing much was said
about the fear of David during
that time, but he was human,
not God, so no doubt he had
some fear," I add.

"I mean, as humans standing
in front of a mighty predator,
capable of crushing you, is a

cause for concern to anyone."
You nod, eyes still open with
wet prisoners. "But," I say
while slipping a tear off your
face with my right thumb,
"David was the underdog, he
bet on his courage and skillset.
He won because his size wasn't
important in a decisive fight he so
wanted to win." You nod, you smile.
I smile. "His skillset was designed to
take out the mighty. One clear shot
was all he needed. He aimed, he fired.
He defeated."

I hold your hands into mine.
"What I am trying to say,
babe, is that you are always going to
be the David in your problems. Even
with fear and tears, and doubt, you
can one-shot your problems because
you are so talented, so brave, you
always bounce back." You smile.
You find my lips, you sniff, you
keep on kissing me. My you.

"Let's go get a drink," I say,
pulling you up.
"Thank you so much," you say again,
your gaze filled with gratitude,
love. You lean in, laughing.

Our lips collide again, and
just like that we've won the rounds,
we have cleared the clouds
with the perks of love and wisdom.

Clarity

When you only have one
life, how you chose to
live it is important. You
make that difference clear
to me. This is why I love you.
The clarity you bring into
my blind spot.

Before you, I had all these
moments, but they
made no difference because
I thought nothing good about
life. I just wanted the ride to
finish when the cassette is
done playing the same soul-wrecking tunes.

But then you arrived,
the tune changed and the
sense of wreckage waned as
my heart tidied into your tide.
You changed the meaning of
my one life, one ride perspective.
You became my new favourite tune.

Now, you are my favourite song,

you are my every moment,
your voice is my playlist and
I don't want us to play out just
yet. You and me, we have two
lives, and now after doing the
quick math, I am glad I paid
attention in class, we now have
double the moments.

Meaning, let's double the fun
and stretch into every
adventure we can think of.
"Are you in?" I ask you.

You smile and softly whisper,
"Yes." Your gaze fixed as ever
into mine with certainty.
I smile.

Distant but Close

At nine a.m. sharp, I sit at
my home office, working
on an architecture project
for a client, and you at yours
across the room. My phone
rings and I pick up. Before
I can introduce myself, I stop.

I smile at the oak floor, I know.
You breathe into the speaker with
the same vibration as always,
never a variation, and I smile.
I don't have to picture what you
are wearing today.

I helped you zip it up before
I left to change out of
my bathrobe into my three-piece suit. I was expecting
visitors, investors.

"I want to hear your voice,"
you say.
"I want to hear your breath,"
I say.
"I miss you," I say.
"I love you," you say.

More

Your lips invite my lips for
a stroll, and my tongue
decides to tag along.
You twist your tongue
like a key into mine, and
my soul opens like a gate.
It is a long and wet stroll,
but it washes our desires
until we feel clear to take
a break.

We take deep breaths,
flushed lushly by the
rush of ecstasy.

*This is what happens when
you have a you like my you,*
I think to myself.

I love you, same as the
first day. I crashed
into you, and you held me.
"I love you more than the more
you love me," I say. You smile.
"That's the beauty of us; you, me,

always more for each other.
You are my more. I am your
more," I say to you. You blush.

You Are My Comfort

The inconvenience of heartbreaks
makes us less amicable to ourselves
and more adaptable to feeling
less of ourselves, but today,
you've taken me out of my struggle,
into your heart.

With every new heartbeat, I
am more than surviving, I
am thriving, I strive. I sit,
staring at you, void of
discomfort, of feeling
more deserving of joy,
of love, of happiness.

You smile, and your gaze
feels like a soft new couch,
settling me into a new kind
of comfort. You give me a
new sense of destination.
Peace.

Darkness Until You

Before you, nothing felt good
for my heart, nothing sparked
my soul.

Before you, even when
outside it was bright
and sunny, inside myself
I couldn't feel the warmth
or the glow or any flow at all.
Then you arrived, bringing in
an overflowing glow,
brighter than any sun,
fuller than any moon,
showing me a way out
of my abyss. I crave
you like my own heartbeat.

The Yearn

After so many years,
we still yearn for one another.
We have both aged, but
nothing of value has changed:
our heart still carries the
energy of our youth, the
allure of eternal love. It's
like your beauty is frozen,
defying the curse of time,
and my love for you is still
held in captive.

This is what I love about you
and me, and us, the rebellion
against society, against nature.
Aren't we a symbol of eternity?

You carry the blessing of a
goddess, all the flawless
features and weightlessness
of life's essence.

No Masks

Over the years, I have seen
you in many greys and
colours, all of them well-fitted over your mood. All
of them sexy AF.

You have shown me your
demons, and I have dined
with them in their fancy
dresses. I have opened
my closet, too, and you
have tidied the rags on
my skeletons, making me look
as handsome and wholesome
as never before.

You have seen my clouds
and closet, and I have seen
all the many moods of your
sky, and still we've stood side
by side, no matter our past storms.

I Will Do Anything for You

I will fall in love every day
for you, with you.

I am glad that we are
now more than an arrangement,
we are an attachment.
No schedule necessary,
we just live life without
the burden of time.

You make me want you
more and more. I am
filled to the brim with you,
but I am designed to
hold any more you
decide to become. Love
carved me into a bowl
to hold you in, no matter your ocean.

I curl my fingers around
the nape of your neck, and
you light up like candlelight, your
eyes showing me every dark
delight of your caved soul,

inviting me into an arrangement
of surfeit mischief.

At our new townhouse,
I stand at the window pane,
watching raindrops attack
the defensive window, unable
to hear the soothing soft
drumming of its beating,
but it's okay. I have a better
sound keeping my soul alive.
My heart, beating in tune to
the voice of your soul.

I smile as you steal my
attention without being
present through the earplugs
in my ears. You speak, and
I listen to your voice.
"Chapter five," you say, reading
from one of your best sellers.
Your words, your voice, the
little breath I can hear you
take in-between the words.
My breath mingles with my
smile. I love you in all your
gracious talent.

You touch me, and I look
at you standing so close
to me, a silky sheet wrapped

around you, instead of your
clothes splattered at the bottom
of the bed. You want to stay.
Confirmed. I smile.

Judicial Merging

Looking through the
outline of our memoir
since you became the
very source to my beating
heart, I am convinced that
we are ripe for an engagement.

We have progressed from
individual protege to one
perfect package, bound by
love and pulled forward by it.

Today, I realised that love is
a flow. It starts with an
encounter, then an
arrangement to merge
two into one adventurous
living.

It is an entailment of
contentment, commitment,
development, adjustment,
entitlement and enchantment.

These sacrifices demand

a judicial merging, a marriage.
But first, we have to get the
engagement out of the way,
I thought that night, while in bed,
watching you sleep peacefully.
I think about the glint in
my jacket suit, hanging in
my dark closet.
I smile like a diamond.

As One

A glint in my palm,
goosebumps on my skin,
you on your heels, me
on my knees. It is no surprise
why your gaze catches
mine with a frown from
where I am crouched.

I can feel your thought,
just the same way I feel
the sunny heat against my skin.

And yes, you are right,
I am about to do what
I am about to do, I say
with my eyes. You smile.

Your eyes glint, diamond-bright.
I wear your big
gaze like a ring and it fits
perfectly. The only right
size for me.

I nod as if I understand
what your eyes are saying.

Yes, this one moment will
change everything we've
done until now. You
confirm with the tears of
joy flowing down your
cheeks like rain drops from
the sky.

We all have something
to offer but the big question
is what are we willing to
sacrifice to get it?
I remember you asking
me that question one night,
when we had one of our
can't-sleep, all-nighter bed
talk times. I don't just want to
be an offer, I want to be
a sacrifice. I want to
sacrifice myself for what
love demands, for you.

Two-in-One Sky

My heart beats like a
boombox against my
chest, loud with my love
for you. I take one millisecond
to admire the one thing that
has brought me this much
joy today. Love.

Love is like day and night
under one sky, like rain and
sunshine under one sky,
like grey and rainbows
under one sky. Like you
and me under one sky.
Love is a sky.

Today

It is a warm morning,
the sun is out, the birds
are chirping, as if they've
just eaten the best worm in
their lives. I am hungry for
you, my you, and I can't
wait to become a happier
chap, after chirping my
vows to you.

The wind blows, and my
mind floats into the future
where we become balanced
as one against the imbalances
of life.

I always feel the need to
think about what tomorrow
might bring, what I wish it to bring.

But today is where I must
do something about it.
For this is what love demands,
thinking and doing, vision and
action, preparation and

expectations. I know that
love isn't always easy, but
it carries a weightless breeze
to ease the weight.

You are my balance,
you've shown me a parallel
stance during my fiercest
burden. You've quenched my
doubt over the years like an
ocean soaking in every
burning ship that crosses its path.

I want us to be husband
and wife, an ally and a family.
A yes is all we need to seal
the deal.

The very first day you
happened to me, I knew
we had hit it off, because I
smiled so big that it hurt
my cheeks.

As soon as you nod
your head, my fingers
find yours and roll the
ring into the perfect one.

You glance at its glint, and
your gaze dances like a

ceremony. I am healed.

"I want to hear you say it
aloud," I say. "I am hot for
you," I add, still on one knee,
my heart booming.
You are worth a shot,"
you say, still on your heels.

"Does that mean a yes?"
I ask. Your gaze meets
mine, blooming like flowers.
"The biggest yes of my life!"
you exclaim. One palm pressed
against your chest, surprised, excited.
The other stretched out under
the bright sky.

The birds chirp even louder,
probably rejoicing, joining in,
in this fine goldmine.

Suddenly, like broken
wings, we fall again into
one another and rebuild.
Like parts of a new plane,
we became welded together
and ascend into the
brightest blue sky. Marriage.

Final Act

I have been up now for
hours, watching you take
delicate breaths. It soothes
me to see how peaceful
love is in flesh form.

My mind strays back to
yesterday at the altar, and
I smile a million watts.

It feels like only seconds
ago when our vows became
one, when our soul became
strong as we had that final
'yes' to eternity.

I remember your smile,
your gaze, every second it:
your lips parted and joined
mine like a magnetic force,
and we froze the moment
with our first marital kiss.

You tilted your head back as
I stretched my tongue into

the reach of yours. Your
tongue interlaced into mine
like a lover's fingers on a stroll,
and our families whistled
and clapped and cheered.

It was the final act to seal
the deal like a pact. "Love is
a wolf," I remember you
whispering into my ears.
"It has led us to this wonderful
moment," you said. "Now
look at me, looking at you."
"Thank you, love wolf," I said
with one whispery breath.
You yawn and turn towards me.

My Tomorrow

I watch you as you open
your eyes and turn toward
me. "Morning, my gorgeous
wife," I say. You rush a
hand through your bedhead.
You smile.

"Morning, my handsome
husband. I am glad to be here now
with you," you say, as you
open your eyes further.

"I am glad to know that
I will wake up tomorrow,
and you will be the one
on the other side of my
bed," I say.

"I can certainly get used to
these morning romances,"
you say.

"I have plenty where that
came from," I say. "It enhances
our day."

"It sure does," you agree.

"You, my darling, are my
new path in life. We're past
the part of no return," you say.

"Yep, you are stuck with
me now," I say. You smile.
I can tell by your gaze.
It burns through all the
bridges that lead back
to my hurt past. "My heart
beats for now and tomorrow
for you," I add.

Happy Harvest

I kiss you and a smile stretches
itself across your lips.
You kiss me back, and I
am filled full like an
empty glass. Giving others
your every minute so they
can be happy is like giving
the rich your every penny
so they can stay rich,
while you stay poor. But
with you, each time I give,
I am enriched. With you,
each minute loving you
is an investment.

With you, it's different;
with love, it is different.
You reciprocate what's
given, you enrich me with
the same effort. And on my
cloudy days, you make wine
of my whining like was
made with the waters at Cana.

This makes me thank Jesus

for bringing you into my life,
for changing my heart from
its drawn waters of exes, by
bringing you to me, and
making you mine, my divine
wine, now my divine wife.

You always find a way to
take what's long given
and like a garden of soil,
you multiply it ten folds and
give it back in love folds.
You are my happy harvest.

Soulful Memory

We fought last night, and
we lost a precious time, but
we woke up looking for
peace. I ease in next to
you on the couch, and
you slip me a smile.

I look at you, and my
mind flashes back to
our wedding day, our
voices filled with promises
under the devoted sky as
your yes intertwined with
my loud vow.

Your smile melts into
mine. You stretch out
your hand bringing me
back to this moment and
my gaze settles into yours.

*What's divine can't be
divided,* I remember my
vows. *Few words, but every
word I meant. And this*

moment, isn't it the aim
of it all? Sticking together
no matter how sticky the
situation gets? I think to
myself. And in an instant,
everything eases away.

The truth is, in chaos,
we are always one memory
away from peace. Often
when I get anxious and
worry about things, I remind
myself that life has thrown
us against the wall plenty
of times, and we have
bounced back each time.
Each scratch only a tiny
stone compared to our wall.
Our love.

This time won't be
any different. As I look
at your face, I realise
once again that the sight
of you brings millions of
wonderful soulful memories
to the surface. I lean over,
and I kiss your lips.

Passion

I inhale you, your sweet
scent, before you step
towards me. I scoot over,
making room for you.
"I drew a sketch of you.
Look," I said, turning the
canvas around as you slide
on the bench on our porch.
Your face lit up by the moon,
hovering above the sky
like an open book.

You sketch me a beautiful
smile around your lips,
better than the one I drew
of your lips on the canvas.

"Your drawing is always
Nikon precise," you say.
"My dimples, my collarbone,
my tiny silver nose piercing,
my black lace bra—everything
sketched like a mirror."

"Love breeds passion,

and passion breeds
precision," I say.
"So, love is a pattern of
progress?" you ask
teasingly, pleased.
"Yep," I nod.

"But do you want to
know a secret," I say.
You nod. "With art, you don't
have to be precise,
you just have to be
passionate. Passion
catalogues precision,
and precision comes
with sufficient love for
something. I have
enough of it right
here in front of me.
You."

"Easy, my love-struck
philosopher! Is it the
moon? Is your heart
turning into a werewolf?" you tease.
"Maybe it's the moon mixed
with pheromones," I say.
You smile, amused, your
lips leaving nothing of
sparse.
"You are more cheesy

when you can't sleep,"
you say.
We both smile as we
look up at the pitch-black sky.

You run your feet over
my bare legs. Your toes
feel warm and boneless
against the July's night breeze.

"Let me show you something,"
you say. You unlock your
phone, illuminating our faces
like chandelier lights,
calling forth your Facebook.

"These are among my
very best art," you say,
as the photos of our
honeymoon uploads.
"It was a wonderful time,
let's frame our walls with
them, babe," you add. I smile.

"You are right, babe," I say
in my architect demeanour,
"I want every wall to be our
alibi, our own memory box,"
I add, letting my hand hover
across the air, visualising the
view.

Toughest Storms and Strength

Today, you made
dinner, and the scent
fills my heart.
You do know the
way to my heart.

You pull me by my
tie, and I follow you
without a fight,
staring at you, in
all your glorious
steps and shape.

Your heels click
across the marbled
floor, and my cufflinks
shine against it.

I drink your view
in like a strong shot
of smooth, dark gin.
I grin. My you.

It has been a long day
at work, but you are

my best kind of project.
I am an architect.
I have to build what's
unstable, I have to
erect what I have neglected.
You.

I sit down, and you
smooth your skirt and sit
down next to me.

We both breathe in the
aroma of delicious food
hovering above us.

"What's the occasion?" I ask.

"Reconciliation," you whisper.

"I am an author. I decide
how this night ends,"
you add. I smile.

"I see! In that case, I
won't waste another
twilight on a fight with
you or another sunlight
without a fight for you,"
I say with an aura of delight.

"Nope! I won't let you, even if

you weren't ready for peace.
So, none of us is going
to bed angry tonight,"
you say.

"Neither of us is going to
bed hungry either," I say,
smiling.

"This morning, we went
to work angry.
Tonight, we will go
to bed affectionate, like lovers.
Like the good and bad and
naughty and grateful husband
and wife we are," you say.
We both smile.

This is what marriage does,
it backs us into a corner, but you
are never alone when the bell
rings to get back into the ring,
when it's time to face the fight,
I think to myself.

You are my team, and I
won't switch sides, not today,
not tomorrow, not ever, I
think to myself again. You smile.
You must know my thinking pattern
by now, my you, my partner

in crime.

My mobile buzzes, and
I ignore it. You pick
it up and stretch it toward
my gaze. I
grab it, turn it off and toss
it far away from you,
erasing it from the
ease of this peaceful
moment. From our
peaceful setting
tonight. I smile.
You smile.

I look at the table,
and I wow. "I am
super proud of you,
but your lips aren't on
the menu," I say. You
gaze, and it sparkles
against the glint glow
of the ceiling bulb. Red glow.

I lean in and give you
a kiss. You smile.
Seeing you smile
always reminds me
that we enjoy
the strength of our
own joy.

I look into your eyes, and
I see you. "I don't want to
wake up next to no one
else," you say.
"I don't want to sleep knowing
that you are with another
one's ex," I say.

We smile like lovers,
like soldiers fighting on one
team against a common enemy.
You are my ally, my team,
and love is our weapon.

We fought against one
another like war enemies
last night, like few other times
before, and now we are
fighting for us like every
other time. We have
ridden back to our base,
to our senses. We know,
because we smile in unison.

Love is a rollercoaster,
and sometimes, you
just don't want to ride
any more. You want to
get off, and go home. Alone.
But not when you are in love.

Not when you mean it. Not
when you've given all of you
into the one for you.

"We've seen many
dark days together,
we've escaped many
caves together. We've
been at our lowest points,
climbed our highest
mountains. We've
glowed through our
growth. We've come
out brighter," you say.

"We've seen ourselves
sick of one another,
and we've recovered
like sick patients.
I vow to continue to
value you, accept you,
love you, entertain you,
need you, trust you,
involve you, never
lie to you, evolve with you," I say.

You smile as you tug
a strand of blonde hair
behind your ears. Flattered.

That's how I want

you to always feel
next to me. "Let's eat
now," you say, flushed,
all shy and pretty.
A smile swims across
your face as you fill my
jug from our tall glass
of water. My butterflies
fly to the top of your sky.

Grey to Greener

Today, you are grey and
our sky isn't bright. My
you, my green grass, gone
grey. Neglected even
without intent. But I am
at fault. I admit.

The only thing that rises
and seems of no value is
smoke, the same goes for
lovers' quarrel. I can't stand
not seeing your smile each day.

And it's true like you wrote
in one of your thrillers, that
what you can't stand is only
what changes, everything
else is just a smoke, lame,
useless, temporal, quick to
rise, but designed to exit
and extinct, permanently.

You are not a lustful wish,
you are my love, my life,
my after the day's destination,

no matter the miles covered.

I have been working too
much lately, forgetting
my chores: love, and my
responsibility you. It is
true, the neighbour's grass
isn't self-colouring.

Effort makes the grass
greener. Sometimes, I did
wonder why mine isn't
as green as usual, as green
as the ones you see on
Instagram or Facebook and
its kinds, but then I usually
see my neighbour in reality,
outside my window, early at
dawn, before the first
bird chirps, before the
first cock crows, at work
when everyone else lies
awaiting the rain to fall,
even in the hottest summer
like every other year for
decades.

It is not a special kind of
water that the neighbour
uses. It is effort, I realise.
And so, I take the day off,

phone off and put my
gardening mood on and
a nice song on; it's time
to get busy the old-fashioned way. Love.
Accountability. Reparation.
Responsibility. This is my
way of self-redemption.
Of righting what hasn't been
done right.

I get to work. "It's my turn
to take care of you," I say.
At my instruction, you put
your feet up and your
shoulders fall free. At
your direction, I pour you
a glass. At your specification,
I mix the ingredient.

You smile at the aroma of a
delicious meal, as your feet
soak in bubbles. "Did you
take up massage classes?"
you exclaim as my fingers
release your shoulders of
stress with a gentle massage
and your empty ears are
filled and your heart overflows
with all the lovely words
in the dictionary of lovers.
Again, love wins.

My You

Every moment with you
is a pleasure, loving you,
being loved by you.
My you.

My ride or die,
my highs and hurricanes,
my rainbows and rains,
my sun and sunset,
my waves and tides,
my hand in hand,
my side by side.
You are a giver of grace.
My heart beats daily,
just to see your smile.

Last Flame

The music spreads
evenly around
us like smooth confetti.
Side by side, we
lie down under
our silk sheet,
warm and comfy,
your fluffy socks on,
your last wish.
It has been a long
bold ride.
I can tell.

I look at the
machine beeping,
its wires running into you.
I look back at you and sigh.
My hair is grey,
but your head is bald.
"Cancer, what have
you done to my you?"
I say softly to you as
I look into those
blue eyes riddled
with concern.

You close your eyes,
take a deep breath.
Suddenly, you smile like the
very first day you
tripped into me.

You open your eyes, and
I catch your gaze
and fold my hands
gently around your
delicate body, once
firm but nevertheless
still hot, like a burning fire.

"Are you okay?"
I ask.

"I feel perfectly
fine given what
time I have left,"
you say.

"You do know
that death comes
in many ways to
claim us all one day?"
you ask.

I nod a yes to you.
Painfully. You smile,

prettily. You inhale me.
"I have always loved your
perfect smell," you say. "I
wonder if they sell any
of it up there when I get
there," you joke.

"You never let the worst
get the best of you," I say.
I smile.
"You've still got it in you.
You've always lived lively no
matter the dread. Death
must hate you right now
for being bold in the face
of it. It made you bald
but it was never able to take
your bold, I think to myself," I say,
face wet with sadness.

"Death is very
creative, you know.
I mean look at me,
bald and fray, in pain,
drained of energy,"
you say slow and soft.

"You look fabulous
to me," I say.
"Death is a time
machine, it takes

us back to every
moment that we
had, that we made or
didn't make count," I add.

"When I closed my eyes,
I was counting them but
I stopped counting our
memories," you say.

I nod in agreement and
I smile. "I too stopped
counting them, there are
way too many," I say.
You part your lips slowly
and smile sincerely.

I just want to enjoy
this very moment and
count more memories
of you, of us later,"
I say.

You lean in for a
kiss, and our lips touch.
I light you one last
time like one lit
candle to an unlit candle.
You flicker, and
I flame like old times.

Our souls stand tall
beside one another,
our flames swaying
delightfully, taking
in one last wind
before you burn
down for the last time.

Slowly, you sway with
pain and more discomfort.
I can feel the life leaving
your once-lively body. You
look towards the wall. I
do too. Emotions begin
to melt down
my cheeks as we
both smile at all
the adventures
framed and hanging
on our walls.

You smile, and it
is the second
best memory I will
remember of you.
The first best memory
is every other time before
today.

Before You

Even at this last, sad happy hour,
my heart is as high for you as
it was the first time we met.

Before you, my heart stood
still, void of hope to feel
love for myself, for another.

My butterflies were laid down
inside the pit of my stomach,
strangled by heartbreakers.

Before you, my soul felt unable
to crawl, unable to stand,
unable to walk, unable to jump
at the mention of love.
But your smile makes my heart
do backflips, your voice
makes my soul fly high.

Vows

"You know how to bring
out the best in any moment,"
you say to me.

"You give me too many
credits like the ones you
see at the end of a
movie, but you know who
really made the story worth
it? You," I say as my hand
brushes over your head, one
last time as if you still had
your pretty blonde hair.

"Love is a vow of two souls,
for better or for worse, we
must continue in love. This
is my best moment, the grace
to see you for one last time,"
you say.

"This is my worst moment,"
I say, knowing that it would
be my last time seeing you
breathe. But our vow binds
me to carry on for you, for us.

Alibi

You inch a bit closer, and
our faces are parallel from
where we lay.
"The perfect love story
doesn't exist, except
fairy tales such as
Cinderella, *The Little
Mermaid*, *Beauty and
the Beast*, *Sleeping Beauty*,
Snow White, *Aladdin*,
Frozen, *The Frog-Prince*,
etc. Audience love,
spotlight love," you say.

"We never needed
audience love, spotlight
love," I say.

"I know we didn't have
the perfect love story,
but our love never
regressed. We had the
necessities; we had love,
we had clarity, we had
certainty, we had passion,

we had respect, we had loyalty,
we had discovery,
we had pheromones,
we had a pattern, and
we progressed.
This is the definition of a
fairy tale, the memory.
The many tales framed
on the wall, our wonderful
adventure is our alibi," you say.

Indefinite

"You are a memory that
can't be washed away
by the greatest depth of
any big ocean, indefinite.
A picture that can't be
destroyed on earth or in
heaven, indefinite.

Even six feet under, even rotten
within my skin, even
stripped naked to my
vulnerable bones, even
crunched and crushed
by flames to ashes, my
memory of you will stay
surfaced on my face for
as long as the sun stays
above the Earth.
You are my indefinite,"
you say with a million-miles smile.

"I love this brakeless moment,
this speed of spell,
this last magic hour,
this last-minute ride of romance.

I love this stained ride
of smiles on your face,
this highway of love, doing
over the speed limits,
feeling immortal, even though I
will crash when it all stops,
even though I am bleeding
before the final crash," I say.

"Despite broken, despite
bleeding and needing
you to stay a little longer,
starting the romance a little
further, your foot on the pedal,
my gaze on your windows,
my heart beats a billion
times alive," I say, "hoping
that in your last minute, it
stays permanent with the
rest of what's indefinite about
me in your wonderful heart," I add.

One Breath Away

I look into your eyes for
what feels like an eternity,
and I know when your
mind is occupied with
something important.
You take a deep breath and
your mouth opens slowly.

"Before you, love was
anything but love; frantic,
tragic, it was nothing in
comparison to everything
we have—magic. And now,
looking at everything one
last time, it is ironic how one minute
your whole life ahead of
you can be right in front
of you. How what's left of it
can be only moments away—
only one happiness or sadness away,
only one regret or redemption away,
only one single breath away.
Spending my last breath with you,
in your embrace, in your graceful presence,
on all our lovely memories of a loved
life is the most satisfying way
to spend this one last breath," you say.

Eternal Beauty Sleep

You inch even closer to me
and our faces, now one hot
breath apart. I feel my heart pulse,
and the rush of the blood
pumping through my veins.

"You are a life well-spent,"
you say to me in
one last breath.
"You are my life,"
I say to you.

"I love you,
always," you say
to conclude your
farewell.

"I love you
more than always,"
I say back at you.

You smile your best
smile, your last smile.
"Goodbye, my you,"
I finally say as you

close your eyes
to your first
eternal beauty sleep.

Throwback

I look at you for one last
time, and I see your
trademark smile. The one
that gave a million reasons
to fall in love with you in a
millisecond. The one that
made my heart spin like
a roulette.

Even in your peace, you
look like a pretty goddess.
What a badass! My you.
Perhaps, it is your way of
telling death to go to hell,
on your way to heaven.

I take in a deep breath and take
in your favourite perfume.
It flushes me back to a throwback.
That day when I looked
at your pristine face for the
first sight under the skylight.

I remember looking at you
and my heart unleashing and

my gaze running through the
features of your face. I looked
at you, and your face was a
commanding beauty, crystal
to its core, carved
clear as a glint glass.

Now even with everything
that has happened in this hour,
your beauty is still as mesmerising.
And now it has become clear
to me, you are a ruler of all
beautiful things.

Even in death. You are
extraordinary, you make
angels look ordinary.

Final Thought

You've made me realise
that we all go through
pain because we hunger
for what's real, and each
breakup builds us up for
the real lasting love.

It is true that refusal does
not mean failure. Delay
does not mean forever.
You taught me to be patient
in my search, in my progress,
that what is mine took so
long because time designs
great things to last! And
when the time is ready to
give us what's ours, it will
make sense each and every
other day afterwards. Timing
presents love and makes
love memorably eternal.